SPIRITUAL DISCIPLINES

SOLITUDE
SILENCE

BIBLE STUDIES

Jan Johnson

6 STUDIES WITH NOTES FOR LEADERS

IVP Connect
An imprint of InterVarsity Press
Downers Grove, Illinois

Inter-Varsity Press
Nottingham, England

InterVarsity Press
P.O. Box 1400, Downers Grove, IL 60515-1426
World Wide Web: www.ivpress.com
E-mail: email@ivpress.com

Inter-Varsity Press, England
Norton Street, Nottingham NG7 3HR, England
World Wide Web: www.ivpbooks.com
E-mail: ivp@ivpbooks.com

InterVarsity Press® is the book-publishing division of InterVarsity Christian Fellowship/USA®, a movement of students and faculty active on campus at hundreds of universities, colleges and schools of nursing in the United States of America, and a member movement of the International Fellowship of Evangelical Students. For information about local and regional activities, write Public Relations Dept., InterVarsity Christian Fellowship/USA, 6400 Schroeder Rd., P.O. Box 7895, Madison, WI 53707-7895, or visit the IVCF website at <www.intervarsity.org>.

Inter-Varsity Press, England, is closely linked with the Universities and Colleges Christian Fellowship (formerly the Inter-Varsity Fellowship), a student movement linking Christian Unions in universities and colleges throughout the United Kingdom and the Republic of Ireland, and a member movement of the International Fellowship of Evangelical Students. For information about local and national activities write to UCCF, 38 De Montfort Street, Leicester LE1 7GP, email them at email@uccf.org.uk, or visit the UCCF website at www.uccf.org.uk.

All Scripture quotations, unless otherwise indicated, are taken from the Holy Bible, New International Version®. NIV®. Copyright ©1973, 1978, 1984 by International Bible Society. Used by permission of Zondervan Publishing House. All rights reserved. Distributed in the U.K. by permission of Hodder and Stoughton Ltd. All rights reserved. "NIV" is a registered trademark of International Bible Society. UK trademark number 1448790.

Cover design: Cindy Kiple
Cover and interior image: Digital Vision

U.S. ISBN 978-0-8308-2097-9
U.K. ISBN 978-0-85111-697-6

Printed in the United States of America ∞

 InterVarsity Press is committed to protecting the environment and to the responsible use of natural resources. As a member of the Green Press Initiative we use recycled paper whenever possible. To learn more about the Green Press Initiative, visit <www.greenpressinitiative.org>.

P   25   24   23   22   21   20   19   18   17   16   15   14   13   12   11   10   9   8   7   6   5

Y   29   28   27   26   25   24   23   22   21   20   19   18   17   16   15   14   13   12   11

CONTENTS

INTRODUCING
Solitude & Silence

Have you ever wondered how God changes people? Maybe it seems as if old habits never change no matter how hard you try. Maybe you've become discouraged with your lack of growth into Christlikeness. You know that you are forgiven through Jesus' suffering on the cross, and you realize that you are totally accepted by God on that basis. This is wonderful. And yet your desire to live in a way that pleases God somehow constantly falls short of the mark.

God desires to transform our souls. This transformation occurs as we recognize that God created us to live in an interactive relationship with the Trinity. Our task is not to transform ourselves, but to stay connected with God in as much of life as possible. As we pay attention to the nudges of the Holy Spirit, we become disciples of Christ. Our task is to do the connecting, while God does the perfecting.

As we connect with God, we gradually begin acting more like Christ. We become more likely to weep over our enemies instead of discrediting them. We're more likely to give up power instead of taking control. We're more likely to point out another's successes rather than grab the credit. Connecting with God changes us on the inside, and we slowly become the tenderhearted, conscientious people our families always wished we'd become. This transformation of our souls through the work of the Holy Spirit results in "Christ in you, the hope of glory" (Colossians 1:27).

God does in us what we cannot do by being good. Trying to be good generally makes us obnoxious because it's so obvious that we're only trying. The goodness doesn't come from within ourselves. When we do succeed at being good, we subtly look down on those who don't do as well. When we don't succeed, we beat ourselves up and despair over our lack of spirituality. Either way, we remain focused on self instead of on setting our hearts on things above.

Connecting with God, then, is important. But what does connecting with God look like? Through the work of the Holy Spirit, we copy Jesus in behind-the-scenes, everyday activities he did to connect with God. As we let these activities become habits, we slowly become "trained" to have the heart of Christ and behave as he did. These activities are spiritual disciplines, also called spiritual exercises or strategies.

How Spiritual Disciplines Work

We connect with God through spiritual disciplines or exercises. Solitude and silence, the topics of these Bible studies, are two of them. Other disciplines include community, submission, Bible study, Scripture meditation, worship, celebration, prayer, listening, service, secrecy, reflection, confession, fasting and simplicity. These exercises are studied in the other Spiritual Disciplines Bible Studies. Still other disciplines can be used, some of which are written about in the classics of the faith and others God will show you. Henri Nouwen said that a spiritual discipline is anything that helps us practice "how to become attentive to that small voice and willing to respond when we hear it."*

---

*Sources for quoted material can be found at the end of the guide.

How do spiritual disciplines help us connect with God?

- They build our relationship with God as we acquaint ourselves with the ways of God. (It's possible, of course, to do these disciplines in a legalistic way and never bond with Christ.)

- They build our trust in Christ. Some of the disciplines are uncomfortable. You have to go out on a limb. You try fasting, and you don't die. You serve someone, and it turns out to be fun and enriching.

- They force us to make "little decisions" that multiply. Your little decision to abstain from watching a television show helps you to deny yourself and love others in all sorts of ways.

- They reorganize our impulses so that obedience is more natural. For example, if you have a spiritual discipline of practicing the presence of God, you may learn to automatically pray the breath prayer "Into thy hands" when someone opposes you. Without your realizing it, your opponent is no longer an adversary, but a person God is dealing with or perhaps even speaking through in some way.

- They help us eventually behave like Christ—but this is by God's miraculous work, not our direct effort.

- They teach us to trust that God will do the work in our inner being through the power of the Spirit (Ephesians 3:16). Your spirituality is not about you; it's the work of God in you. You get to cooperate in God's "family business" of transforming the world.

How We Get Spiritual Disciplines Wrong

Spiritual exercises must be done with the goal of connecting, not for any sake of their own or any desire to check them off a list of "to do" items. If you read your Bible just to get it done, or because you've heard this will help you have a better day, you'll be anxious to complete the Bible study questions or to get to the bottom of the page of today's reading. But if your goal in Bible reading is to connect with God, you may pause whenever you sense God speaking to you. You'll stop and meditate on it. You may pray certain phrases back to God, indicating your needs or your wishes or your questions. You may choose to read that passage day after day for a month because God keeps using it to speak to you.

After such a session, you will have a stronger desire to connect with God. That "little choice" you made to connect will leave you slightly different for life.

The exercise or discipline is beneficial because it helps you practice connecting with God. If you want to play the piano well or swing a tennis racket well, you have to practice certain exercises over and over. Good baseball players train behind the scenes by practicing their batting day after day, with no crowds watching.* That's what spiritual disciplines or exercises are about. If you can hear God in fasting and simplicity, you'll more likely hear God in a board meeting or an altercation with a recalcitrant teen when passions run high. In life with God, we get good at connecting on an everyday basis by devoting time to developing the skills needed.

The Disciplines of Solitude and Silence

Solitude and silence are disciplines of abstinence. We abstain from accomplishing the things that make us feel worthwhile (especially completing that to-do list), and we rest in the fact that we are of great worth to God, even when we do nothing. We surrender the need to talk, to fill the empty air with clever thoughts. In the absence of all this puzzling and planning, wheeling and dealing, we meet our true

---

*This comparison originated from and is expanded in Dallas Willard, *The Spirit of the Disciplines* (San Francisco: Harper & Row, 1988), p. 3.

selves. Often this is not pretty. Thoughts we never knew we had come to the surface.

To take time for silence and solitude means we assume that God wants to speak to us and relate to us in a personal way. This is such a stretch for those of us who think of prayer as an exercise in nonstop talking. Instead, we learn to converse with God and hear God—first in the solitude, then in all of life.

How Do These Studies Work?

The studies in this guide examine the reasons, examples and attitudes of these disciplines in our lives. Each session includes several elements.

Turning Toward God presents discussion or reflection questions and exercises to draw us into the topic at hand.

Hearing God Through the Word draws us into a study of a related passage of Scripture with questions that connect it to life and invite us to reflect on what God is saying.

Transformation Exercises are activities or thoughts to experiment with in order to experience the spiritual exercise studied. At the end of the study, look at these exercises and choose the one that fits you best, according to your personality or your current needs. Think of a time to try it on your own and report back to the group the following week.

Perhaps you'll read the exercise and think it's too elementary or too difficult for you. Adapt it as needed. Or maybe you think you can guess what you'll experience, so you don't have to do it. The point is to experience it. Go ahead and try.

Using These Studies in Retreats

These studies work well for an individual taking a personal retreat. Simply do the studies at your own pace, and do not rush them. Allow enough time to do the transformation exercises as well. Don't feel you have to do all the studies. In fact, you may wish to focus only on one discipline and use only those studies.

A group wishing to explore certain disciplines can also use one of these studies the same way. Be sure to allow time for participants to do the transformation exercises. Some exercises may be done as a group. Others may be done individually, with group members reporting back to each other about how they heard God during the exercise.

For either type of retreat, allow plenty of time for pondering. May these studies help you move a few steps closer to living your life in union with God.

1

EXAMPLES OF SOLITUDE

Jesus' Personal Getaways

MARK 1:21-39

If you picture Jesus' day-to-day life, it's easy to imagine him among crowds of people who were trying to get his attention or listening to him as they sat on a hillside. Yet one of the central pictures of Jesus in the Gospels is the solitary figure going off to be alone with God.

Some may wonder why Jesus would need a pattern of private getaways while living on earth as a human being. Hadn't he already spent eternity in fellowship with the Father? This puzzled even the disciples, who are portrayed in the Gospels as having to find Jesus when he had gone away to pray. People have said he did it primarily to set a marvelous example for us today. But his urgency and frequency hint at something better—he sought solitude simply because he longed to be alone with God.

Another startling dimension of Jesus' pattern of solitude is that he took time alone in spite of being a "people person." Unlike John the Baptist, Jesus was not a loner living in the desert. He attended parties, surrounded himself with an entourage of disciples and mixed constantly with crowds. Jesus loved to be with people, and he loved to be alone with God.

Turning Toward God

What moments of aloneness have you enjoyed at any time in your life? Swinging on a swing set in a park as a child? Taking a shower as a teen? Commuting to work without the ringing of the telephone?

"It was an important day in my life when at last I understood that if [Jesus] needed forty days in the wilderness at one point, I very likely could use three or four."

DALLAS WILLARD

In the past, how have you felt during times alone with God?

- awkward
- hopeful
- this is for sissies
- nurtured
- dutiful
- this is for *spiritual* people
- other:

- bored
- confused
- this is for loner types
- such times are too loose
- such times are too rigid
- can't get enough of it

Hearing God Through the Word

Read Mark 1:21-34.

1. If you had been Jesus, what activities recounted here would have exhausted you? *all of them*

Which ones would have exhilarated you?

all of them

---

2. What emotions might you have felt after healing Simon's mother-in-law? (Keep in mind that Simon Peter could have been called Jesus' best friend.) *– fulfilment at*

being able to help a friend

Read Mark 1:35-37.

---

3. Consider your own pattern of sleep after an exhausting day of service. Why do you suppose Jesus did not sleep late the next morning? *He was eager*

to be with God for restoration for the coming day.

---

4. Since it was still dark when Jesus left the house, what inconveniences (such as dampness) might he have experienced in getting off to a solitary place?

"Turn your loneliness into solitude and your solitude into prayer."

ELISABETH ELLIOT

What does this tell you about Jesus' desire to have solitude?

It was essential to him that he do it.

5. Why is it important to stop and reflect with God after hectic times of service?

→ Calms you + help you put the past activities in perspective And refuels you for the future.

How do you usually debrief or clear your head after such times? (Do you talk with a friend? take a walk? engage in vigorous exercise? go to a movie?)

Work crossword puzzles.

"In silence, God pours into you a deep, inward love. This experience of love is one that will fill and permeate your whole being. [It] is the beginning of an indescribable blessedness."

MADAME
JEANNE GUYON
(WHO SPENT
MORE THAN
TWENTY YEARS
IN PRISON
AND EXILE)

6. If you had been Jesus, what topics relating to the day before would you have prayed about?

The encounter with the unclean spirits/demons.

7. What do you find inconvenient or uncomfortable about solitude and silence?

I basically enjoy it but get bored after a prolonged time.

Read Mark 1:38-39.

8. How did Jesus respond to being found and interrupted?

He said let's get on with the day.

How do you explain this, especially his statement "That is why I have come"?

He knew why he was on earth and wanted to accomplish all he could while he was here.

9. How does this passage encourage you to understand the helpfulness of time alone with God?

If paint out that Jesus needed time alone with God how much more do I need it.

10. What do you think is the difference between solitude and loneliness?

_____

11. If you were to have a personal retreat day or morning, where would you go and what would you do?

Transformation Exercises

Experiment with one or more of the following.

• Reread Mark 1:21-39. Which moment in this story speaks most to you? Sit and imagine yourself in that moment. What about that moment would you like to integrate into your life?

• Walk around your bedroom, apartment, house or backyard. Where could you sit with no distractions? What could you do to make it easier to focus in that place—move a bench or rocking chair there? turn a chair toward a window?

• Start a file folder for a personal retreat day. Place a blank sheet of paper in it. As you move through your days, write on that sheet any passage of Scripture that begs to be pondered. Toss in the folder any magazine articles that you'd like to ponder. Next to the folder, set books through which God has spoken to you in the past.

• Think back to a recent day full of service (or a week-by-week program you're involved in). Pray about this time of service, commenting to God on what startled you or pleased you. Ask God to offer other insights regarding the day.

• If you already spend a lot of time on your own, seek out a different place of solitude away from your usual habitat, such as a public park or walking down a quiet street.

2

EXAMPLES OF SOLITUDE
Jacob's Transformation

GENESIS 28:10-22; 32:22—33:3

Sometimes we stumble upon solitude, and other times we intentionally create it. Two events in Jacob's life illustrate this. In the first, Jacob stumbled upon the presence of God in a solitude that was forced upon him as he fled from his brother's threats of murder. In the second scene, Jacob chose solitude (to scheme, or to hear from God?—we don't know). And God "showed up" in an unforgettable way.

In both solitary scenes, Jacob was haunted by fear of his brother Esau. Jacob had lied to his father to get a blessing intended for his brother (following the instructions of his mother, who most likely thought she was acting in accordance with God's prophecy in Genesis 25:23). That was why Jacob fled. The second occasion was Jacob's homecoming—would Esau still be angry?

Jacob's encounters with God in solitude show us how solitude is not just for the supposedly spiritually elite. Even re-morseless people find help in solitude. For Jacob, these encounters and others became stepping stones to a life devoid of manipulation and full of love for God and pur-pose in life.

Turning Toward God

What usually causes someone to say, "I need to be alone to think"? When, if ever, has God met you in solitude around a specific challenge in your life?

Hearing God Through the Word

Read Genesis 28:10-22.

1. What promises and reassurances did God give Jacob during Jacob's dream at Bethel (vv. 13-16)?

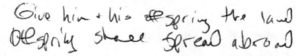

2. Why would a person who has lied and manipulated as Jacob had need to hear this message?

3. When have you thought, "Surely the Lord is in this place, and I was not aware of it" (v. 16)?

"We in our 'existence as usual' are like Jacob, wearily asleep on our rock in our own desert ravines. Jacob went to sleep in his sorrow, alienation, and loneliness, seeing only the physical landscape. In his dream—or was he only then truly awake?—he beheld the commerce of God, and awakening cried out: 'Surely . . .'"

DALLAS WILLARD

Read Genesis 32:22—33:3.

---

4. What was clever about Jacob's strategy of making sure Esau would see his family (long-lost relatives) and his many possessions before Esau faced Jacob himself?

Send the children out first.

---

5. The prophet Hosea later described Jacob's struggle this way: "He struggled with the angel and overcame him; he wept and begged for his favor" (12:4). What does that add to this picture?

---

6. A common experience in solitude is to recall a certain person who is an adversary or challenger and criticize that person. If we consciously invite God's presence, a shift may occur. God confronts *us* about our character or our need to die to self and trust God completely. How would this shift change the way we pray in solitude? Give some examples below.

Prayers of a Person Who Fears Someone or Opposes Someone	Prayers of a Person Who Is Being Confronted by God
God protect me against	*God help me to see as you do*

"*They will question you saying, 'What are you looking for, what do you want?' To all of them you must reply, 'God alone I see and desire, only him.'*"

THE CLOUD OF UNKNOWING

What does this reveal to you about how you might pray differently?

_____

7. Considering Jacob's character, why was it appropriate for God to appear as a wrestler to Jacob?

_____

8. The "man" renamed Jacob "he struggles with God" (Israel) instead of "deceiver" (Jacob; Genesis 27:36). If God were to rename you (based on a positive change in your character), what would you like your new name to be?

Verity

"It requires a lot of inner solitude and silence to become aware of these divine movements. God does not shout, scream or push."

HENRI NOUWEN

_____

9. How was having a limp in his leg an appropriate memento for Jacob/Israel? (We don't know if the limp was lifelong or temporary.)

_____

10. How did God remedy the situation with Esau without Jacob's having to manipulate it?

11. If you ventured into solitude, which of Jacob's solitary experiences might yours more closely resemble—Jacob's first one of encouragement and comfort or Jacob's second one of being challenged? Which one do you need most? Which one do you think *God thinks* you need most? Why?

12. How did God use solitude to transform Jacob's soul?

In what ways do you hope the practice of solitude might change you?

Transformation Exercises

Experiment with one or more of the following.

• Imagine Jacob lying beside the Jabbok River, which was about thirty feet wide and hip-deep. It probably made some bubbling or swishing sounds and was very calming to Jacob that night. Are there certain sounds that help you in your practice of solitude—for example, sitting by a river or ocean, listening to wordless music, tuning in to bird calls or wind chimes?

• Journal regarding your character flaws and the way God

has been leading you to change your character. Start by listing them on the left side of the paper. Then to the right of each one, list a form in which God might appear to you in a dream or in your thoughts. Choose a form that would correspond to your flaw, as a wrestler corresponded to Jacob's flaw of manipulation. For example, if one of your character flaws is self-pity, perhaps God might "appear" to you in the form of a mourning dove or a whining child.

• Pray, offering two requests, as Jacob did as he wrestled with "the man" (to bless him; to tell him his name). Let one include the new name you think God would like to give you. Interact with God in prayer about this.

3

ACTIVITIES IN SOLITUDE
Delighting in God

PSALM 37:1-11

Many people view God primarily as a problem solver, the Great Therapist in the Sky. When this is true, we use psalms to soothe ourselves in times of trouble. As we learn to love God for who God is, we enjoy God more. We learn the important skills of waiting on God, being still before God, and delighting in God, meaning that we love God, are thrilled by God, and can't keep our minds off God.

This new attitude changes the way we approach passages such as the well-known verses of Psalm 37. Before, we may have thought that if we delighted ourselves "in the Lord" (paid some spiritual dues of praise), God would give us the desires of our hearts (an upbeat attitude, an attractive body, a car that never breaks down). We delighted in the Lord to get God to give us stuff. But as we instead learn to treasure the person of God, God becomes the desire of our hearts.

Psalm 37 is often considered a comfort psalm, but it also shows us concrete ways of trusting God: delighting, waiting and being still. These are a few of the how-to techniques of solitude. Learning them ensures that our solitude and silence with God are not empty. Waiting on God and being still is not a tiresome ordeal for the super-holy. It is full of interaction with God. We can look forward to it with expectant alertness.

Turning Toward God

What do you find particularly satisfying or meaningful in life?

"Center all your attention and desire on [God] and let this be the sole concern of your mind and heart. Nourish in your heart a lively longing for God."

THE CLOUD OF UNKNOWING

Hearing God Through the Word

Read Psalm 37:1-6.

1. Based on the commands in verses 1-2, what did the psalmist assume his hearers were going through?

2. The command to "dwell in the land" implies that the hearers expected the worst and planned to run away from the evildoers. What does the psalmist say they should do instead (v. 3)?

3. If you were to "delight in the Lord," what aspects of God (what God is like, how God acts/evidence of God) would you treasure?

4. Imagine that you know some people who obviously delight in the Lord. Why would it be easier to see goodness (righteousness) in them or to see the fairness of their causes (v. 6)?

5. Why would it be easier for a person who is fully committed to God to delight in God, wait on God and be still before God?

Read Psalm 37:7-11.

6. What are some practical ways you can still yourself before God when you're irked that wickedness seems to be winning?

"For the man or woman who has come to know and love the Lord God in the depths of such intimacy, the times of solitude are the most precious in all of life. They are a rendezvous with the Beloved. They are anticipated with eagerness. . . . Gentle interludes with [God] alone are highlights of life."

PHILLIP KELLER

7. What is the wisdom behind the spiritual adage, "When in doubt, wait"?

8. In what situations do you need to walk away in order to refrain from a display of anger?

"When Thou dost knock at my heart's door, let me not keep Thee standing without but welcome Thee with joy and thanksgiving."

JOHN BAILLIE

9. Many times it seems that those who "possess the land" (RSV) or "inherit the land" (NIV) are the ones who have grabbed it successfully. But what sorts of people does this passage say will actually secure the land?

10. Find the two places in this passage in which the word *enjoy* occurs. What attitudes or actions bring on enjoyment?

11. How do you think a person who has learned to wait on God, delight in God and be still before God would be different from others?

12. Reread Psalm 37:1-11 aloud slowly. Which word or phrase is most meaningful to you? Why?

What does that phrase tell you about how you want to connect with God?

Transformation Exercises

Experiment with one or more of the following.

- Sit in a quiet place and read the following verse:

> The LORD your God is with you,
>   he is mighty to save.
> He will take great delight in you,
>   he will quiet you with his love,
>   he will rejoice over you with singing.
> (Zephaniah 3:17)

What song do you need for God to sing over you?

- Extend the palms of your hands out in front of you. Imagine that in your hands you hold someone who irks you or a troublesome situation. Illustrate what this passage has urged you to do with these troubling situations by moving your hands in some way. (Some examples: dumping out their contents, tossing away the contents, gently putting the contents down somewhere safe and walking away.) What is God urging you to do?

"We need to find God, and he cannot be found in noise and restlessness. God is the friend of silence. . . . We need silence to be able to touch souls. The essential thing is not what we say, but what God says to us and through us."

MALCOLM
MUGGERIDGE

- Try doing a physical activity such as taking a walk or riding a bike or gardening and in some way delighting in God at the same time. Don't try too hard or worry about doing it perfectly. Just try it. When your mind wanders, pull it back gently to God's goodness in your life.

- Study the connections between waiting and hoping as they are linked in passages such as Psalm 33:20; 130:5-7; Lamentations 3:24-25; Romans 8:23-25. How are waiting on God and hoping in God related? What does this tell us about the nature of waiting on God?

4

ACTIVITIES IN SOLITUDE
Resting in God

ISAIAH 30:15-22

Let's say you decide to sit for a few minutes in solitude and silence. To most people this signals one thing—sleep! If drowsiness doesn't overtake you, another obstacle looms: the list of all the things you should be doing. (You can put them to rest by jotting them down on a pad.)

It's never surprising when the first few minutes of quiet prayer or the first hours of a private retreat must be spent ushering distractions to the door. You may have noticed that an entire "distraction committee" lives in your head. Members of this committee vary but often include

• *Looking Good Kid,* who says to you: "Excel! Be smart! Look great! Achieve, achieve, achieve!"

- *Rescue the World Crusader,* who says to you, "Help folks to the extreme, even if they don't want it."

- *Critic,* who scolds you and evaluates everyone around you, saying, "Why aren't they doing what's right or what you want?"

- *Leisure Junkie,* who says to you: "How long until your favorite TV program? Why don't you stop and get a doughnut, or ten doughnuts?"

Inviting these inner committee members to leave (a gentle approach works best) is a primary skill needed to hear God in solitude and silence. What we're aiming for is silence within, quietness in the soul.

"When you come to the Lord, learn to have a quiet mind. Cease from any self-effort. In this way, God himself can act all alone," wrote MADAME GUYON. Wise souls will find it a relief to no longer be "pleasantly attached to their own efforts."

Turning Toward God

When your mind is racing with thoughts, what are they usually about? What do you do to quiet these thoughts?

Hearing God Through the Word

In this session's passage Isaiah prophesies to Judah, a nation in the midst of crisis. Assyria was threatening to overrun Judah. Would the people of Judah turn to God for help or put their confidence in human help (particularly Egypt)? They were full of hurry and panic. God told them to rest, to be quiet and to wait. Then they would hear God.

Read Isaiah 30:15-17.

1. What means of finding salvation and strength does Isaiah recommend?

2. How are these means the opposite of what a panicked person often does?

_____

3. What kinds of things does a person of quietness and trust "put to rest"?

_____

4. What evidence of panic do you see in the lives of the Judeans (vv. 16-17)?

_____

5. Think of a situation that usually rouses panic in you. If you took time to rest and be quiet before God (or habitually did so and therefore your response would come from that), how would you respond differently?

Read Isaiah 30:18-22.

_____

6. What do these verses tell us about how God feels about us—even when we panic?

"I am becoming aware that with words ambiguous feelings enter into my life. It almost seems as if it is impossible to speak and not sin."

HENRI NOUWEN, AFTER SPENDING THREE MONTHS AT AN ABBEY WHERE SPEECH WAS LIMITED

7. How can the assurance that God loves to show grace and compassion and to bring about justice make us more likely to wait on God?

8. What does Isaiah say would be God's response to the people's cries for help (vv. 19-20)?

9. In what ways do you experience the phenomenon described in verse 21?

___ remembering the words of helpful teachers

___ receiving holy nudges through a sense of rightness, based on what we've been taught

___ hearing God within the heart

___ other:

10. What specific form of obedience did Isaiah prophesy would occur if Judah heard God as described in verse 21?

11. Why would a life of constantly hearing God (as described in v. 21) make people want to give up whatever distracts them from God?

12. How can quietness and rest help us hear God?

Transformation Exercises

Experiment with one or more of the following.

• Reread Isaiah 30:15-22 and pick a phrase that describes the kind of life you'd like to have. Repeat that phrase to God, and sit quietly in God's presence and enjoy the prospect.

• Journal your own down-to-earth paraphrase of Isaiah 30:15-22. Rephrase verse 15 as needed. Then rewrite verses 16-17 inserting your sources of hurry and panic. Rephrase verse 18, and replace verses 19-20 with what you believe might be God's response if you waited on him. Rephrase verse 21, then replace verse 22 with an act of radical obedience that might result.

• Sit for a while in silence and ask God this question: What do I need to know? Don't force an answer, but wait quietly. If nothing comes, simply enjoy God, focusing on what you love most about God when distracting thoughts come.

• Try being silent for a period of time as you go about your business (a whole hour, a whole morning, a whole day). If your situation requires you to speak, say as little as possible. Try going without any background noise such as a radio or television. If you think this will bore or isolate you, keep a Bible open to Isaiah 30:21 and read it occasionally.

5

RESULTS OF SOLITUDE
Hearing God's Surprises

1 KINGS 19:1-18

After her daughter died, my friend began making a silent retreat every year. Each time she gained amazing insights and experienced spiritually uplifting moments. But in the fourth year, her retreat seemed dry. She read Scripture as usual, but she felt disappointed and let down. Four odd things came to mind. She needed to eat properly (instead of snacking so much), get more exercise (besides her old routine), get more sleep and stop trying to get sleepy by watching so much TV late at night. She wrote these things down and waited for more. Nothing came—where were the "spiritual" insights?

After the retreat, she felt disappointed, but she implemented those four changes, one at a time. She found that her perspective changed in amazing ways. "I realized my spiritual part was not a separate part of who I am," she said. "God is concerned with every detail about me." With these changes, she found it easier to receive from Scripture and to sense God's presence.

This is a common experience with God. In solitude God "shows up" in surprising ways, often with uncommonly practical insights. In this passage Elijah has similar experiences in solitude with God. After Elijah infuriated Queen Jezebel by upstaging her false prophets and calling down fire from heaven, she threatened him with death. Fleeing from her, Elijah was greeted with God's tender practicality and brilliant ability to show him what he needed to know.

Turning Toward God

Share an experience of being surprised by God.

Hearing God Through the Word

Read 1 Kings 19:1-8.

1. Why does Elijah flee to the desert and on to Mount Horeb? What is he seeking?

2. What sorts of character traits are formed in a person who relies so heavily on the protection, guidance and companionship of God?

3. How did the angel choose to respond to Elijah's hope-
   lessness (vv. 5-8)?

Read 1 Kings 19:9-18.

"If I have not
developed and
nurtured this
devotion of
hearing [as
Samuel had when
he said, 'Speak for
Your servant
hears'], I can only
hear God's voice
at certain times.
At other times I
become deaf to
Him because my
attention is to
other things—
things which I
think I must do.
This is not living
the life of a child
of God."

OSWALD
CHAMBERS

4. Why do you think the all-knowing God would ask,
   "What are you doing here, Elijah?"

5. Which of the following attitudes do you detect in Elijah's response?

   ___ wishing God to be honored

   ___ whining about his state

   ___ self-righteous in his actions

   ___ self-pitying in his aloneness

   ___ wishing a carnal vengeance on the idolaters of Israel (possibly a showy one such as more fire falling
   from heaven, see 1 Kings 18:38)

   ___ rebuking God for allowing such miserable circumstances to continue

   ___ others:

6. How does God's "gentle whisper" (v. 12) compare with
   Elijah's previous experiences with God (1 Kings
   18:24, 38) and Moses' experiences in this same place
   (Exodus 33:21—34:10)?

7. How do you respond to God's choice to use the "gentle whisper" to communicate with people?

8. What do you learn about human encounters with God in solitude from the fact that after God spoke in the gentle whisper, God repeated the same question to Elijah, and Elijah gave the same answer (vv. 9, 13)?

9. What do you make of God's belated comment about the many people in Israel not devoted to Baal, though Elijah had insisted he was the only faithful one left (v. 18)?

10. What do you learn about solitude with God from God's practical instructions to Elijah in verses 15-18?

11. If you were to run off to be with God in a place of historic holiness (as Mount Horeb was), what do you think (or hope) God would offer you?

___ rest

___ nutritious food

"The longer I walk in faith and consistently acknowledge my beloved Spouse by waiting on Him in silence, the more I 'hear' Him and sense His leading in the details of everyday life. Now, instead of agonizing over every situation, I rest in Him, aware of His involvement in the myriad of daily decisions, and excited beyond imagination about each new day as it unfolds."

BILL VOLKMAN

__ conversation

__ opportunities to release honest thoughts and feelings

__ ideas for future service

__ ideas for whom you need for companionship

__ other:

Transformation Exercises

Experiment with one or more of the following.

• Imagine a tempest, earthquake or fire in the terrible solitude of a mountain pass. Journal or talk with a friend
about how you would have felt during this natural phenomenon (breathing hard, covering your face, hiding in
the dark of the cave). Then write or tell about how you
would have responded to the gentle whisper.

• Choose a specific place where you love to be alone. Plan
a time when you can be there for a while.

• Sing a song about solitude (such as the hymn "In the
Garden") as you are driving, or hum it quietly while
riding the bus.

• Figure out all the details that would need to be addressed in order for you to have a few hours alone
somewhere. For example, find out when people in your
household will be out (or could be, or could take others
with them) or when a certain solitary place is available.

6

RESULTS OF SOLITUDE
How God Changes You

JOHN 15:1-16

Folks sometimes view solitude and silence as me-myself-and-I practices. They think, *You do this to make you feel warm and close to God.* But besides helping us enjoy God's presence, a steady habit of solitude and silence changes the way we behave toward others. The two great commandments are inseparable: to bask in the love of God results in a quiet but powerful love for others (Matthew 22:37-39).

When I first began having snatches of solitude, I found myself feeling grouchy when my kids interrupted. Or when I returned from times of solitude, I dreaded the noise and chaos. It took practice to let this sense of God's nearness flow back into the clamor of family life.

Yes, there's a shift when we move from the peacefulness of solitude to the chaos of relationships, but solitude affects our relationship with God *and* our relationships with others. In solitude God speaks to us about the people we love (and those we don't) through prayer, Scripture reading, journaling and so on. God draws us toward them. God uses solitude and silence to change us—we bear fruit, obey difficult commands and offer others selfless, Christ-driven love.

Enjoy this peek at a discourse in which Jesus explains that as we do the connecting, God does the perfecting. As we abide in Christ, we bear fruit of loving obedience. This bonds us as friends of God, and the abiding becomes more automatic.

Turning Toward God

Why is it sometimes easy to feel that we love God but still be a little annoyed with someone in our life?

Hearing God Through the Word

Read John 15:1-10.

1. The dual theme of John 15:1-10 is "to abide" (NRSV, NKJV, or "remain," NIV) and "to bear fruit." Consider what it means to abide or remain in Christ. What would abiding look like in your life?

2. What does "bearing fruit" mean in this passage?

3. If God were to use solitude and silence to prune your soul, what challenges might God present to you in the quiet atmosphere of overflowing love?

---

4. If God were to use solitude and silence to cultivate your spiritual life, what truths might God want to make real to you—because you don't fully accept them with all of your being? (Here are some ideas to get you started.)

___ You are loved, no matter what.

___ Knowing God is delightful; he says, "Taste and see that I am good."

___ God has a redemptive purpose for your life.

___ Other:

"The sole purpose of solitude is knowing God, and those who know God will care for God's children. . . . It is out of solitude, out of being authentically present to God, that the deepest care for God's creatures comes."

DAVID
RENSBERGER

---

5. For obedience (loving enemies, caring for the have-nots, telling the truth) to be possible, what needs to be in place in our lives (vv. 5-6)?

---

6. If a person abides in union with God, why might their prayers normally be answered "yes"?

7. What personal insight about obedience and survival does Jesus give us about himself (vv. 9-10)?

Read John 15:11-16.

8. What results occur for the person who lives in union with God?

"*Solitude molds self-righteous people into gentle, caring, forgiving persons who are so deeply convinced of their own great sinfulness and so fully aware of God's even greater mercy that their life itself becomes a ministry.*"

HENRI NOUWEN

9. In what way is the battle to love others waged in solitude and silence on one's knees?

10. What reasons might we give for hesitating to think that God would ever call a human a "friend"?

How could we answer those doubts?

11. If you had a personal retreat day (or "Friendship Day with God"), what pitfalls (obstacles to be pruned) might trouble you?

___ I would structure it so much that I would have a difficult time hearing God.

___ I would put off doing it.

___ I would goof off all day.

___ I would fill the day with tasks from my "to do" list.

___ Other:

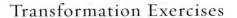

12. What format for solitude and silence works best for you? (Taking a walk? Going to a retreat center?) How, if at all, are you motivated to expand that?

Transformation Exercises

Experiment with one or more of the following.

• Describe in your journal a mental picture or a sensory image that would represent what it means to abide in God. Or make a photo album or video diary of these images. Here are some examples.

God singing or humming over you, perhaps rocking you (Zephaniah 3:17)

squatting in the shadow of God's wings (Psalm 36:7; 63:7)

"Without a certain element of solitude there can be no compassion because when a man is lost in the wheels of a social machine he is no longer aware of human needs as a matter of personal responsibility. . . . Go into the desert, not to escape other [people] but in order to find them in God."

THOMAS MERTON

> riding behind God on a majestic horse on behalf of truth, humility and righteousness (Psalm 45:4)
>
> drinking from and romping in God's river of delights (Psalm 36:8)
>
> gazing on God's beauty; dwelling in God's house (Psalm 27:4)

• Set aside a period of time for silence and solitude. Pray for someone who is difficult or who has opposed you. Ask God to show you this person's heart.

• Think forward to a conversation you'll be having (lunch with a friend, a break at work, after dinner with your child). Purpose that for five minutes you will be "slow to speak and quick to listen." You will drink deeply from that person's words, without jumping ahead mentally to what you want to say next or what your opinion is of what they're saying.

• Take a hymnal, sit in a swing and sing all the hymns you can find that have the word *abide* in them. You can start with "Abide with Me" or "Beneath the Cross of Jesus."

GUIDELINES FOR LEADERS

My grace is sufficient for you. (2 Corinthians 12:9)

If leading a small group is something new for you, don't worry. These sessions are designed to be led easily. Because the Bible study questions flow from observation to interpretation to application, you may feel as if the studies lead themselves.

You don't need to be an expert on the Bible or a trained teacher to lead a small group discussion. As a leader, you can guide group members to discover for themselves what the Bible has to say and to listen for God's guidance. This method of learning will allow group members to remember much more of what is said than a lecture would.

This study guide is flexible. You can use it with a variety of groups—students, professionals, neighborhood or church folks. Each study takes forty-five to sixty minutes in a group setting.

It's true that getting people to discuss the Bible requires some thought. The suggestions listed below will help you encourage discussion by paying attention to group dynamics.

Preparing for the Study

1. Ask God to help you understand and apply the passage in your own life. Unless this happens, you will not be prepared to lead others. Pray too for the various members of the group. Ask God to open your hearts to the message and motivate you to action.

2. Read the introduction to the entire guide to get an overview of the issues that will be explored.

3. As you begin each study, read and reread the assigned Scripture passage to familiarize yourself with it. Read also the focus statement at the beginning of the notes for that study, which appear later in this section.

4. This study guide is based on the New International Version of the Bible. It will help you and the group if you use this translation as the basis for your study and discussion.

5. Carefully work through each question in the study. Spend time in meditation and reflection as you consider how to respond.

6. Write your thoughts and responses in the space provided in the study guide. This will help you to express your understanding of the passage clearly.

7. It may help to have a Bible dictionary handy. Use it to look up any unfamiliar words, names or places. (For additional help on how to study a passage, see *How to Lead a LifeGuide Bible Study* from InterVarsity Press.)

8. Consider how you need to apply the Scripture to your life. Remember that the group members will follow your lead in responding to the studies. They will not go any deeper than you do.

Leading the Study

1. Begin the study on time. Open with prayer, asking God to help the group to understand and apply the passage.

2. Be sure that everyone in your group has a study guide. There are some questions and activities they will need to work through on their own before, during or after the study session.

3. At the beginning of your first session together, explain that these studies are meant to be discussions, not lectures. Encourage the members of the group to participate. However, do not put pressure on those who may be hesitant to speak during the first few sessions. You may want to suggest

the following guidelines to your group.

- Stick to the topic being discussed.

- Base your response on the verses studied, not on outside authorities such as commentaries or speakers.

- Focus on the passage of Scripture studied. Only rarely should you refer to other portions of the Bible. This allows for everyone to participate on equal ground and for in-depth study.

- Anything said in the group is considered confidential and will not be discussed outside the group unless specific permission is given to do so.

- Help everyone get involved by limiting your responses if you contribute a lot or by responding more if you're usually quiet. But don't feel forced to speak up.

- Listen attentively to each other and learn from one another.

- Pray for each other, especially if you feel that someone is struggling with an answer. Praying is better than interrupting.

4. Have a group member read aloud the introduction at the beginning of the discussion.

5. Every session begins with a "Turning Toward God" section. The questions or activities are meant to be used before the passage is read. These questions introduce the theme of the study and encourage group members to begin to open up. Encourage as many members as possible to participate, and be ready to get the discussion going with your own response.

6. Have one or more group member(s) read aloud the passage to be studied.

7. As you ask the questions under "Hearing God Through the Word," keep in mind that they are designed to be used just as they are written. You may simply read them aloud. Or you may prefer to express them in your own words.

There may be times when it is appropriate to deviate from the study guide. For example, a question may have already been answered. If so, move on to the next question. Or someone may raise an important question not covered in the guide. Take time to discuss it, but try to keep the group from going off on tangents.

8. Avoid answering your own questions. If necessary repeat or rephrase them until they are clearly understood. Or point out something you read in the leader's notes to clarify the context or meaning. An eager group quickly becomes passive and silent if members think the leader will do most of the talking.

9. Don't be afraid of silence in response to the discussion questions. People may need time to think about the question before formulating their answers. Count to twenty before rephrasing or commenting.

10. Don't be content with just one answer. Ask, "What do the rest of you think?" or "Anything else?" until several people have given answers to the question.

11. Acknowledge all contributions. Try to be affirming whenever possible. Never reject an answer. If it is clearly off-base, ask, "Which verse led you to that conclusion?" or again, "What do the rest of you think?"

12. Don't expect every answer to be addressed to you, even though this will probably happen at first. As group members become more at ease, they will begin to truly interact with each other. This is one sign of healthy discussion.

13. Don't be afraid of controversy. It can be very stimulating. If you don't resolve an issue completely, don't be frustrated. Explain that the group will move on and God may enlighten group members in later sessions.

14. Periodically summarize what the group has said about the passage. This helps to draw together the various ideas mentioned and gives continuity to the study. But don't preach.

15. Every session ends with "Transformation Exercises." At the end of the study, have a participant read them aloud. Then ask each participant to choose the one that fits them best, according to their personality or current needs. Ask them to tell the group which one that is and a time they could try it.

    Before the next session starts, ask whether any participants tried the transformation exercises. You might lead into this by telling about one you tried. So-called failures really are not failures. These things are a matter of skill building. You never learn to ride a bike unless you get on it the first time and keep trying.

16. Conclude your time together with conversational prayer, adapting the prayer suggestion at the end of the study to your group. Ask for God's help in following through on the commitments you've made.

17. End on time.

Many more suggestions and helps can be found in *The Big Book on Small Groups* (from InterVarsity Press).

STUDY NOTES

Session 1. Examples of Solitude
Jesus' Personal Getaways
Mark 1:21-39

Focus: When Jesus, Son of God yet very active human, came to earth, he spent time in solitude and silence with God.

Turning Toward God. Use one or both of these questions to warm up participants to this topic. In the second question, it may help to own up to your shortcomings by telling of your limited ideas about solitude.

Question 1. Many of these activities may have exhausted Jesus: having people hang on to every word because he taught with such authority (being popular can be exhausting!); the physical exhaustion of teaching so authoritatively; the shock of being interrupted by a screaming possessed man; the dismay of being identified so well so publicly so early in his ministry; the demands of having the "whole town gathered at the door"; the grief at seeing so many people who had been ravaged by disease and demonic possession; the pressure of keeping those demons quiet about his identity.

Question 2. Consider these possibilities: the tears and emotionalism of Simon's mother-in-law and her family, whom Jesus may have known very well since he often stayed in Capernaum; the solicitous gratitude Peter may have felt and kept expressing.

Question 4. Other inconveniences might have been not disturbing anyone (or being detained) as he left the house; finding his way in the dark; being cold and shivering because the sun wasn't yet shining; perhaps being very hungry if he left without eating anything.

Question 5. Often we don't reflect because we're so tired. Yet reflection time can be fun—praising God and expressing those "Gee whiz!" feelings; expressing questions of fear and uncertainty; offering prayers for ongoing healing in people's lives.

Question 6. Possibly Jesus prayed for people's ongoing healing. He may have prayed for the discernment of Peter and the other disciples upon receiving a very personal miracle. Since word of him was spreading through his home region of Galilee, he may have prayed for his precious home folk and the many world travelers who passed through along the trade routes of Galilee. Maybe he prayed for friends and neighbors in Nazareth. Or perhaps Jesus let himself be filled up with the love of God—which would have made him more energetic and ready to serve, as shown in the text.

Question 7. If you wish, refer back to the second question in "Turning Toward God" for ideas. If participants identified with some of those responses, probe more deeply into them.

Question 10. Solitude is the glory of being alone, while loneliness is the pain of being alone. Solitude is being alone with God, so it is not lonely.

Question 11. Listen without commenting. Many people try to be very structured when taking a retreat day, which is not a good idea, but that will be discussed later. Most people feel pretty lost if someone suggests they take a personal retreat. Allow them to express that feeling.

Session 2. Examples of Solitude
Jacob's Transformation
Genesis 28:10-22; 32:22—33:3

Focus: In solitude and silence, Jacob finally stopped trying to manipulate

God and became Israel, who loved God and gave himself to God's purposes. Even very unregenerate people find help in solitude.

Question 1. In the dream, God gave Jacob a "doing" promise—that his descendants would become a great nation that would bless the entire world (through Jesus)—and a "being" promise—that God would be with him and keep him safe.

Question 2. Jacob needed God's protection, and he needed to know his life had purpose even though he had displeased his brother. Even though he began his pattern of manipulation by simply obeying his mother (and she had acted on divine insight; see Genesis 25:23), he apparently developed a penchant for manipulation that would meet its match in his uncle, Laban.

Question 4. Jacob created safety for himself by putting women and children in front of his rugged, brawny brother. Genesis 32:13-22 describes Jacob's presents to his brother and how he planned to impress him with his possessions.

Question 5. This "wrestling match" was more than physical. Jacob wept—a strong show of emotion. He begged for favor, apparently giving up (finally) ideas that tricks or schemes would save him this time.

Who was "the man"? Some say this was an angel, as identified by Hosea (12:4). Others believe it was Jesus because of Jacob's words "because I saw God face to face" (v. 30).

You might ask participants to consider how anyone could overcome a supernatural being. Theologian H. C. Leupold explains this: "This statement does not impugn God's omnipotence, but it does effectively portray the power of prayer. . . . As the will of man learns ever more perfectly to submit to God's will, God can no longer 'prevail' against such a one."[1] Jacob's "winning" may have been not a power match but a spiritual victory enacted in physical terms to give Jacob the lifelong encouragement he would need.

---

[1]H. C. Leupold, *Exposition of Genesis* (Grand Rapids, Mich.: Baker, 1976), 2:877.

Question 6. Instead of begging for God to make our situation okay or wreak vengeance on a person, we ask God to search our hearts, give us grace and lead us in the right path (Psalm 139:23-24).

Question 7. Wrestlers manipulate arms and legs, and Jacob had been manipulating people. A wrestler, then, appealed to Jacob's character and drew him in.

Question 8. If you wish, lighten the tone by rewording the end of the question with, "What would your mother or your roommate or your spouse like for that new name to be?"

Question 9. A limp is a sign of weakness. Weakness is something a clever manipulator (such as Jacob used to be) would never want. But based on the way Jacob's character exhibited greater trust after this, this weakness apparently created a powerful dependence on God in this patriarch of Israel.

Question 12. Through solitude, God communicated to Jacob that he would use him in spite of all the chaos and even horror (potential fratricide) in his family. This built endurance. In the second solitary interlude, God interacted with Jacob in a tangible and believable form, providing Jacob with the peace he was going to need to steer a brood of sons who would become heads of the twelve tribes—deceiving each other and helping each other.

Session 3. Activities in Solitude
Delighting in God
Psalm 37:1-11

Focus: Solitude is not empty but full of expectant alertness. We enjoy God by delighting in God, waiting on God and being still before God.

Turning Toward God. This could be anything from eating chocolate to attending a professional basketball game. Comment on anyone in whom you see that glow. You might even say that this session is about having that sort of anticipation for God.

Question 1. Apparently evildoers were inhabiting Israel or threatening the Israelites. From the moment the Israelites moved into the Promised Land, there always seemed to be people threatening their claim: the remaining Canaanites; the Philistines (and Midianites and Edomites and so on); and finally Assyria and Babylon. The land was the Israelites' sign of promise, and they feared losing it.

Question 3. Some possibilities for delighting in God: being thrilled and preoccupied with God's great love for us, God's thinking us up before time began and planning for us to be "holy and blameless" (Ephesians 1:4-6), God's work in nature, God's work in others.

Question 4. According to Franz Delitzsch, "he who finds his highest delight in God, cannot desire anything that is at enmity with God," and that person's will is thoroughly blended in love with God's will.[2] Those who delight in God are focused on God and not on themselves. Such selflessness makes it easier for people to see righteousness in them, not self-righteousness. This often promotes nonadversarial encounters, which are more convincing than a competitive approach to others.

Question 5. We know that the actions of delighting in God and committing our ways to God are linked because Hebrew poetry isn't about rhyming but about parallelism—saying the same things in many different ways, using different images.

"Commit your way" means "roll your way," implying one should dislodge the burden from one's shoulders and lay it on God.[3] This would make it easier to wait and be still.

Question 6. Focusing on a short phrase of Scripture is helpful. So is turning each chaotic thought over to God, sometimes using one's hands as an outward sign. "Palms up" indicates turning the situation over; palms down

---

[2]Franz Delitzsch, *Commentary on the Old Testament,* vol. 5, *Commentary on the Psalms* (Grand Rapids, Mich.: Eerdmans, 1973), p. 12.
[3]H. C. Leupold, *Exposition of the Psalms* (Grand Rapids, Mich.: Baker, 1972), p. 301.

invites God to give you back his peace.[4]

Question 7. Rushing ahead is full of hurry and panic. It indicates worry and lack of trust. Trusting and waiting work both ways: a trusting person can wait; a person who chooses to wait will find trust easier.

Question 9. Those who hope in the Lord (v. 9) and the meek (v. 11). In the inverted values of the kingdom of God, advantage is gained by those who wait and hope, not by those who seize control or grab power.

Question 10. *Enjoy* is used in verses 3 and 11. The first requires trusting God (and perhaps not moving around geographically in a search for safety). The second speaks of an inner sense of meekness—not having to control circumstances but being at peace with things as they are.

Question 11. They will live without hurry and panic. They will have an inner posture of patience that will be evident in the way they behave. This will help them fulfill Jesus' second commandment: to love others deeply and truly.

Question 12. After you read the question, explain that you'll read Psalm 37:1-11 aloud slowly and give participants a few moments to respond.

Session 4. Activities in Solitude
Resting in God
Isaiah 30:15-22

Focus: Being quiet before God requires that we get rid of distractions and quiet down the "voices" in our heads.

Question 2. A panicked person often hurries and tries quick solutions without thinking. Repentance, rest and quietness help a person to reflect and see what is needed. Trust helps a person turn situations over to God and find wisdom.

Question 3. People of quietness put to rest thoughts that race through

---

[4]Richard Foster, *Celebration of Discipline* (San Francisco: Harper & Row, 1988), pp. 30-31.

their minds—often these are the agenda of the "inner committee members" mentioned in the introduction.

Question 4. They wanted to flee from trouble quickly on horses. But this panicked response would have overestimated the threat. With only one person threatening, a thousand should not have run off. This would have been an unnecessary overreaction.

The flagstaff phrase refers to desolation. Says commentary writer Delitzsch, "The nation, which had hitherto resembled a thick forest, would become like a lofty pine, standing solitary upon the top of a mountain, and like a flagstaff planted upon a hill."[5]

Question 7. Trust grows as we believe that God will act in compassion and justice. With trust in place, we can wait on God more easily.

Question 8. God would provide the necessary support by answering. Also, the "faithful and well-meaning teachers no longer keep themselves hidden because of the hard-heartedness and hatred of the people."[6] Prophets and teachers of Judah who reflected God's heart would come forth and teach when they saw people crying out to God instead of relying on Egypt. They had been in hiding since the time of Ahaz.

Question 10. They would undertake a radical act of obedience—defiling their idols. Idolatry was the continuous chief sin of the Israelites for hundreds of years.

Question 11. Silencing the voices of the "inner committee members"— all those conflicting ideas—removes primary obstacles.

Question 12. Panicked thoughts and hurried actions make it difficult to hear God, who spoke to Elijah in a whisper (1 Kings 19:12). A person trained in quietness can respond to holy nudges more easily.

---

[5]Franz Delitzsch, *Commentary on the Old Testament,* vol. 7, *Biblical Commentary on the Prophecies of Isaiah* (Grand Rapids, Mich.: Eerdmans, 1969), 2:33.
[6]Ibid., p. 35.

Session 5. Results of Solitude
Hearing God's Surprises
1 Kings 19:1-18

Focus: In solitude, God probes us with questions and surprises us not only with answers but with interaction and practical help.

Background. For the context see 1 Kings 18, especially verses 20-46. Jezebel was devoted to the false god Baal and viewed Elijah and the prophets as the cause of the famine the nation had been enduring. Elijah challenged the prophets of Baal to a contest to see which god, Baal or Yahweh, would bring fire down on a sacrifice. God brought down fire on a water-soaked altar in a dramatic way. Elijah then ordered that Baal's false prophets be slaughtered.

Turning Toward God. Let the question settle for a moment and then offer these possibilities: being surprised by God in nature or in the responses of a child to you or a stranger to you.

Question 1. Commentator C. F. Keil insists that Elijah went to the desert "to pour out before the Lord God his weariness of life, . . . not to save his life . . . but to care for his soul, . . . to commit his soul or his life to the Lord his God in the solitude of the desert and see what He would determine concerning him."[7]

Also, Elijah's entire journey is rich in the symbolism of Moses' experiences in the same geographical area. In this same desert, Moses wandered forty years with the Israelites. Keil says that it took Elijah this long "that he might know that the Lord was still the same God who had nourished and sustained His whole nation in the desert with manna from heaven for forty years."[8] Also, Moses spent forty days and forty nights with the Lord, writing the Ten Commandments on tablets of stone (Exodus 34:28).

---

[7]C. F. Keil, *Commentary on the Old Testament,* vol. 3, *I & II Kings, I & II Chronicles, Ezra, Nehemiah, Esther* (Grand Rapids, Mich.: Eerdmans, 1973), p. 253.
[8]Ibid., p. 255.

Question 2. Such a person not only would have confidence but would not be enslaved to wondering what people thought or pleasing the people around him.

Question 3. First, the angel let Elijah sleep. Then, in both encounters, the angel touched Elijah, then urged him to eat. Finally, the angel provided food so nourishing that Elijah traveled forty days and nights on its strength.

Question 4. This question is probably not the scolding rebuke of a parent but simply God's allowing Elijah to express his extreme feelings.

Question 5. All of these possibilities are suggested by one or more commentators. While Elijah seemed to desire to honor God in a pure way, he also seemed to be focused on self. Thus he overlooked his recent encounter with Obadiah, in which this devout believer and palace servant revealed to Elijah that he had hidden a hundred of the Lord's prophets in two caves (1 Kings 18:7-15).

Question 6. Elijah had just witnessed God's bringing down fire from heaven on an altar, and he may have wished God would be more fiery with the false prophets and leaders. William Sanford LaSor translates this Hebrew phrase as "the sound of gentle quietness," or "gentle silence,"[9] while Keil translates it as "a gentle rustling."[10] Keil goes on to say that God wanted to "show [Elijah] that zeal for the honour of the Lord was not in harmony with the love and grace and long-suffering of God." Keil quotes Herder regarding the "fiery zeal of the prophet" Elijah, who "'wanted to reform everything by means of the tempest" but instead learned "the gentle way which God pursues, proclaim[ing] the long-suffering and mildness of His nature, as the voice had already done to Moses on that very spot.'"

Question 7. Those who see God as a fiery being may be surprised and comforted by this. Those who think that God doesn't do much in this world except

---

[9]William Sanford LaSor, "1 and 2 Kings" in *New Bible Commentary*, 3rd ed., ed. Donald Guthrie and J. A. Motyer (Grand Rapids, Mich.: Eerdmans, 1991), p. 345.
[10]Keil, *Commentary on the Old Testament*, 3:258.

whisper quietly might need to be reminded of the fire in the previous chapter.

Question 8. Acknowledge all answers, saying that this repetition baffles readers terribly. Some scholars even think the repetition is a mistake! We expect Elijah to have learned from his encounter that God is capable of all kinds of fireworks and will bring justice at the right moment, but God plans to be gentle and patient for now.

Assuming the repetition is not a mistake, we can learn a lot about solitude. First, God uses it to ask us penetrating questions (over and over) that will bring out both our selfless and our selfish motives. Also, we can expect this conversation with God to be a process and not give us instant answers or relief. Solitude is about having a *relationship* with God, and it is the nature of relationship not to be cut and dried.

Question 9. This "gentle reminder" is perhaps the most characteristic activity of solitude. God reminds us of truths we've forgotten, making us uncomfortable except that he does it so gently. (If the reminder does not come in peace, it might not be from God but from a scolding committee member; see session 4.) God could have metaphorically grabbed Elijah by the collar and said, "Look, you self-pitying know-it-all . . ." but God didn't. God met Elijah's needs. God let Elijah talk. God assigned him some important jobs. But God also told him the truth.

Question 10. First of all, God often gives depressed people (such as Elijah) some jobs to do. (God is also practical, providing rest, food and drink—vv. 6-8.) In Elijah's case, these jobs were three anointings. The first two would have excited Elijah because they moved forward the cause of justice, which consumed Elijah. (These kings would discipline Ahab and Jezebel, and therefore defeat Baal worship.)

The third anointing would have given Elijah some relief. This loner prophet would gain some sense of community through his mentoring of Elisha. Elisha's appointment also let Elijah know that his prophetic work would continue.

These instructions show how God often gives us concrete ideas that are so creative and God-ordained that we would never have come up with them ourselves.

Session 6. Results of Solitude
How God Changes You
John 15:1-16

Focus: Those who abide in Christ not only find union with God, but also bear the fruit of love, joy, peace, patience, kindness, goodness, meekness and self-control.

Question 1. *Abide* appears in verses 4 (twice), 6, 7, 9, 10 (twice). Synonyms for *abide* are *continue, dwell, endure, stand, tarry,*[11] but perhaps the best one is to be "in Christ." This phrase, appearing many times in the New Testament, refers to salvation (Romans 8:1), obedience (being "alive to God" but "dead to sin," Romans 6:11), belonging to Christ's body (Romans 12:5), commitment to the cause of Christ (Romans 16:3, 9), and being sanctified and changed by God (1 Corinthians 1:2).

To dwell in Christ involves developing an awareness of God's companionship, often through solitude and silence, which may include Bible reading, prayer, journaling, worship and other practices.

Question 2. Bearing fruit refers to changes in character and behavior (Romans 7:4-5; Galatians 5:22-23; Ephesians 5:9; Colossians 1:10). Love entails obedience (John 14:15, 21, 23). These concepts are inseparable in these discourse chapters.

Some have insisted that the fruit a Christian bears is the conversions of new Christians. But the above verses speak of character and righteous conduct as fruit. The "new Christians" view would also deny the allegory of John 15. Branches bear grapes, not other branches. The vine bears the branches.

---

[11]W. E. Vine, Merrill F. Unger and William White Jr., *Vine's Expository Dictionary of Biblical Words* (Nashville: Thomas Nelson, 1985), p. 1 of New Testament section.

Question 3. God often challenges us with the need to love certain people more, to work harder, to live with more integrity—to prune our faults and live as Jesus lived. Sometimes God surprises us with a fault no one has brought up for years.

Question 5. Abiding in God must be in place if we are to obey wisely and faithfully. In solitude, we experience an interactive relationship with God, and through this we are drawn into obedience.

Question 6. If Christ and a person are in a mutually abiding relationship, why would the will of the one differ from the will of the other? What could the abiding person want that would be contrary to love, joy, peace and so on? "Their prayer is only some fragment of [Christ's] teaching transformed into a supplication."[12]

It's important that the "answer to prayer" in this verse not be interpreted to be a key to getting what we want from God; instead it's a description of the natural outcome of living in union with God.

Question 7. With our postresurrection view, we see in these words Jesus' explanation of how he could go to the cross. These verses are Jesus' "how I did it" story. Jesus remained in the Father's love, no matter what. Scholars J. N. Sanders and B. A. Mastin say it this way: "The reason for Jesus' joy is his obedience to his Father and the love which subsists between them (v.10)."[13]

Question 8. They live a life of Christ's joy (as opposed to frail human joy); they learn to love others sacrificially; they become friends of God (vv. 11-14).

Question 9. In solitude we can pray for others, especially those who irritate us. It can take some extended time in solitude before we stop asking God to eliminate that person from our lives and begin asking God to show

---

[12]B. F. Westcott, *The Gospel According to St. John* (Grand Rapids, Mich.: Eerdmans, 1978), p. 218.
[13]J. N. Sanders and B. A. Mastin, *The Gospel According to St. John* (London: Adam & Charles Black, 1977), p. 340.

us what we need to know about that person. When we do, God often shows us the needs of our enemies and gives us a heart of love for them.

Question 10. Abraham was called "a friend of God" (Isaiah 41:8; James 2:23). This doesn't mean having a buddy-buddy relationship with God. It is not an ordinary human friendship based on mutuality and reciprocity; it is based on the unending stability of Jesus' choice of me as a friend (v. 16).

We are friends of God, as opposed to being merely slaves. "A slave obeys from fear, and is left in ignorance of his lord's plans. . . . But Jesus throughout his ministry has taken his disciples completely into his confidence."[14] "The relation of the believer to Christ . . . is essentially one not of service but of love."[15]

---

[14]Ibid.
[15]Westcott, *Gospel According to St. John*, p. 220.

SOURCES

Introduction

Henri Nouwen, *Making All Things New* (San Francisco: HarperSanFrancisco, 1981), p. 66.

Session 1

SIDEBARS

Dallas Willard, *The Divine Conspiracy* (San Francisco: HarperSanFrancisco, 1998), p. 355.

Elisabeth Elliot, "Turning Solitude into Prayer," *Cross Point,* Summer 1997, p. 7.

Jeanne Guyon, *Experiencing the Depths of Jesus Christ* (Beaumont, Tex.: SeedSowers, 1975), p. 60.

Session 2

SIDEBARS

Dallas Willard, *In Search of Guidance: Developing a Conversational Relationship with God* (San Francisco: HarperSanFrancisco, 1993), p. 78.

Anonymous, *The Cloud of Unknowing,* trans. William Johnston (New York: Doubleday, 1973), p. 55.

Henri Nouwen, "Deeper into Love," *Weavings,* September/October 1995, p. 25.

TRANSFORMATION EXERCISE ONE

H. C. Leupold, *Exposition of Genesis* (Grand Rapids, Mich.: Baker, 1976), 2:874.

Session 3

SIDEBARS

Anonymous, *The Cloud of Unknowing,* trans. William Johnston (New York: Doubleday, 1973), pp. 48, 47.

W. Phillip Keller "Solitude for Serenity and Strength." *Decision,* August/September 1981, p. 8, quoted in Joyce Huggett, *The Joy of Listening to God* (Downers Grove, Ill.: InterVarsity Press, 1986), p. 64.

John Baillie, *A Diary of Private Prayer* (London: Oxford University Press, 1956), p. 57.

Malcolm Muggeridge, *Something Beautiful for God: Mother Teresa of Calcutta* (San Francisco: Harper & Row, 1971), p. 40.

Session 4

SIDEBARS
Jeanne Guyon, *Experiencing the Depths of Jesus Christ* (Beaumont, Tex.: SeedSowers, 1975), p. 60.
Henri Nouwen, *The Genesee Diary: Report from a Trappist Monastery* (New York: Doubleday/Image, 1989), p. 133.
C. S. Lewis, *The Screwtape Letters* (New York: Macmillan, 1970), pp. 113-14.

Session 5

SIDEBARS
Henri Nouwen, "Deeper into Love," *Weavings,* September/October 1995, p. 25.
Oswald Chambers, *My Utmost for His Highest,* rev. ed. (Grand Rapids, Mich.: Discovery House, 1992), February 13 entry, italics mine.
Bill Volkman, *Basking in His Presence* (Glen Ellyn, Ill.: UnionLife, 1996), p. 111.

Session 6

SIDEBARS
Thomas Merton, *New Seeds of Contemplation* (New York: New Directions, 1962), pp. 52-63, and Henri Nouwen, *Reaching Out: The Movements of the Spiritual Life* (New York: Doubleday, 1975), pp. 37-62, as developed and adapted by David Rensberger, "The Holiness of Winter," *Weavings,* November/December 1996, p. 40.
Henri Nouwen, *The Way of the Heart* (San Francisco: HarperSanFrancisco, 1991), p. 76.
Merton, *New Seeds of Contemplation,* p. 55.

For more information on Jan Johnson's
writing and speaking ministry, visit
<www.janjohnson.org>.
Or contact Jan at
4897 Abilene St.
Simi, CA 93063